# The Fear of Confidence

David Alto

AltoAdvance LLC / Best Week Ever



9 781716 300707

## DEDICATION

*To the entire LinkedIn community, my connections and followers for helping to create a safe place to share, learn and grow together.*

*Without the LinkedIn community I would not have found my true passion for helping others.*

*Thank you*

*Disclaimer – The materials and information presented here are not a substitute for professional psychological counseling. If your situation needs further help, seek the services of a licensed professional counselor.*

# Contents

# INTRODUCTION

Have you ever written an entire book in just under 6 hours, me neither not until today 10-21-2020.

When you have nothing to do on a 6-hour flight home from Orlando to Seattle, along with no wi-fi and the emotions and feelings that are still so very real from that "traumatic" experience of less than 24 hours ago, I guess you do in fact write a book.

I wrote all but the referencing of previous literature on fear and confidence along with adding action plans for you to use, again, no wi-fi, and Covid-19 not really allowing me to share or ask questions of the passenger sitting next to me. The build of this book was all me during that coast-to-coast flight.

I normally get inspired in my surroundings and then post topics on LinkedIn regarding my travels and or life experiences.... but again, I was filled with emotions and the creative juices were flowing and I just had to get it out.

Not too bad for someone who has never written a book before. Ok, I have books in the works, but doesn't everyone sitting at their laptop at Starbucks have a "book in the works"? FYI, love Starbucks so if you ever see me at a Starbucks, which can be quite often, I will take a Grande Pike with light cream and three sugars. I did tell you this is my first book right? so, I truly do not know how much to share.

I wrote this book to share my experience regarding Fear and Confidence and to help those suffering similar experiences.

I'm going to share the insights of more than a few people. I do truly believe it's fun to promote others while sharing the perspectives of people you know.

I'm going to share my experience with Fear and Confidence and if you wish help you develop a written plan just in case either of those enters your life.

The man pushing a rock up the hill on the books cover does have some significance that I will share with you later in the book.

Ready to get started? Here we go!

# CHAPTER 1

# LEARNING TO EMBRACE FAILURE

I just finished presenting my first ever paid speaking engagement and it was good, except for the first five minutes. This book is the result of that first five minutes and how I embraced my own failure.

Yes, I said it.... Embrace failure

During the moment it sucks.

- Fear of disappointing one's self.
- Fear of being seen as less than a subject matter expert.
- Fear of disappointing others.
- Fear of what your boss or peers or customers will now think of you.

So, why do we fear ...Fear?

Back in the caveman days both women and men had to fear starvation and getting eating by dinosaurs, -well ok maybe they didn't live among dinosaurs but it sure sounded more frightening so let's go with it-.

These are all real legit fears. So, why do we have these fears? Because somewhere, sometime, Grog -our caveman – froze in fear and didn't make a break for the cave, he became a nice little snack for Mr. T-Rex, while his buddies watched.

Fear can take over our entire body. It can shut down our rational thinking, or it can kick us in the ass and encourage us to high tail it away from that T-Rex at Usain Bolt-like speeds.

And yes, this was my first ever paid speaking engagement and I wanted to crush it.

I even practiced it yet again for the, what seemed to be 100$^{th}$ time, at 10pm in the very conference room that I was going to be speaking in the very next day. I even recorded it………… and I crushed it.

So, why in the moment did I struggle with it so much?

Before I discuss why I believe we "mess up in the moment" I would like to discuss how fear works because I believe it will provide an explanation for why fear may be stopping you from the following.

- Is fear keeping you from becoming that entrepreneur you always wanted to become?
- Is fear keeping you from asking for that promotion or raise you know you so deserve?
- Is fear keeping you from attending your first speaking engagement?
- Is fear keeping you from living a fulfilled life?

Let's discuss how fear works on a psychological level, because if you don't know why you have fear, you may just keep fear a very close friend for your entire life, that is not a relationship I want for you nor do you want it for yourself.

In the next chapter I will share with you an article by Theo Tsaousides Ph.D. titled "7 Things You Need to Know About Fear".

Theo writes that eliminating Fear would be the equivalent of taking down your home alarm system because it sometimes makes loud and irritating sounds…. not that practical, right?

# CHAPTER 2

# FEAR

So, let's tackle Theo's "7 Things You Need to Know About Fear"

## Fear is healthy

Fear is hardwired in your brain, and for good reason: Neuroscientists have identified distinct networks that run from the depths of the limbic system all the way to the prefrontal cortex and back.

When these networks are electrically or chemically stimulated, they produce fear, even in the absence of a fearful stimulus.

Feeling fear is neither abnormal nor a sign of weakness: The capacity to be afraid is part of normal brain function.

In fact, a *lack* of fear may be a sign of serious brain damage.

**Can you think of a recent time that fear affected your day?**

**If so please share...**

**Now what did you do to successfully get through your day?**

## 1. **Fear comes in many shades**

Fear is an inherently unpleasant experience that can range from mild to paralyzing—from anticipating the results of a medical checkup to hearing news of a deadly terrorist attack.

Horrifying events can leave a permanent mark on your brain circuitry, which may require professional help.

However, chronic stress, the low-intensity variety of fear expressed as free-floating anxiety, constant worry, and daily insecurity, can quietly but seriously harm your physical and mental health over time.

**What are some things you have done to cope when fear took control of your body and mind?**

**What can you do in your everyday life to implement those answers from the previous page?**

__________________________________________________

__________________________________________________

__________________________________________________

__________________________________________________

__________________________________________________

__________________________________________________

__________________________________________________

__________________________________________________

__________________________________________________

__________________________________________________

__________________________________________________

__________________________________________________

2. **Fear is not as automatic as you think**

Fear is part instinct, part learned, part taught.

Some fears are instinctive: Pain, for example, causes fear because of its implications for survival. Other fears are learned: We learn to be afraid of certain people, places, or situations because of negative associations and past experiences.

A near-drowning incident, for example, may cause fear each time you get close to a body of water. Other fears are taught: Cultural norms often dictate whether something should be feared or not.

Think, for example, about how certain social groups are feared and persecuted because of a societally-created impression that they are dangerous.

**How can you embrace fear and almost welcome its arrival but be able to conquer it in days or even hours or yes...? even minutes.**

**Take a look at how you answered that last question...and ask yourself what can you implement to ensure you embrace fear before it happens?**

### 3. **You don't need to be in danger to be scared**

Fear is also partly imagined, and so it can arise in the absence of something scary.

In fact, because our brains are so efficient, we begin to fear a range of stimuli that are not scary (*conditioned fear*) or not even present (*anticipatory anxiety*).

We get scared because of what we imagine could happen.

Some neuroscientists claim that humans are the most fearful creatures on the planet because of our ability to learn, think, and create fear in our minds. I personally can relate to this statement.

But this low-grade, objectless fear can turn into chronic anxiety about nothing specific, and become debilitating.

**Have you ever suffered from anticipatory anxiety? If so share...**

**What did you do to conquer it?**

_______________________________________________

_______________________________________________

_______________________________________________

_______________________________________________

_______________________________________________

_______________________________________________

_______________________________________________

_______________________________________________

_______________________________________________

_______________________________________________

_______________________________________________

_______________________________________________

_______________________________________________

4. **The more scared you feel, the scarier things will seem**

Through a process called *potentiation*, your fear response is amplified if you are already in a state of fear.

When you are primed for fear, even harmless events seem scary.

If you are watching a documentary about venomous spiders, a tickle on your neck caused by, say, a loose thread in your sweater will startle you and make you jump out of your seat in terror.

If you are afraid of flying, even the slightest turbulence will push your blood pressure through the roof of the plane.

And the more worried you are about your job security, the more you will sweat it when your boss calls you in for even an uneventful meeting.

**Write down any fears you have on paper and be prepared to go into them deeper here soon.**

**Are any of these fears keeping you from achieving your dreams and goals? What are some of those goals that fear is keeping you from accomplishing?**

5. **Fear dictates the actions you take**

Actions motivated by fear fall into four types **freeze, fight, flight, or fright.**

*Freeze* means you stop what you are doing and focus on the fearful stimulus to decide what to do next (e.g., you read a memo that your company will be laying off people).

Next, you choose either *fight* or *flight*. You decide whether to deal with the threat directly (tell your boss why you shouldn't be laid off) or work around it (start looking for another job).

When the fear is overwhelming, you experience *fright*: You neither fight nor flee; in fact, you do nothing—well, you obsess about the layoffs, ruminate, and complain, but you take no action.

Being continuously in fright mode can lead to hopelessness and depression.

**Have you had that Mr. T-Rex fright mode before...if so, write it down so we can address it later.**

______________________________________________

______________________________________________

______________________________________________

______________________________________________

______________________________________________

______________________________________________

______________________________________________

______________________________________________

______________________________________________

______________________________________________

**What are some steps you can take to keep you from having that fright mode?**

___________________________________________

___________________________________________

___________________________________________

___________________________________________

___________________________________________

___________________________________________

___________________________________________

___________________________________________

___________________________________________

___________________________________________

___________________________________________

6. **The more real the threat, the more heroic your actions**

We react differently to real and imagined threats.

Imagined threats cause paralysis.

Being scared about all the bad things that may or may not happen in the future makes you worry a lot but take little action.

You are stuck in a state of fear, overwhelmed but not knowing what to do. Real threats, on the other hand, cause frenzy.

When the threat is imminent and identifiable, you jump to action immediately and without flinching.

This is why people are much more likely to change their eating habits after a serious health scare (e.g., a heart attack) than after just reading statistics about the deleterious effect of a diet based on fried foods.

If you want to mobilize your troops, you have to put yourself in danger.

**Write down when you reacted positively to some type of danger/fear without fearing any consequences.... you just reacted in the moment.**

______________________________________________

______________________________________________

______________________________________________

______________________________________________

______________________________________________

______________________________________________

______________________________________________

______________________________________________

______________________________________________

______________________________________________

**How amazing did that feal.... how empowering did that make you feel and why do you think you felt that way?**

______________________________________________

______________________________________________

______________________________________________

______________________________________________

______________________________________________

______________________________________________

______________________________________________

______________________________________________

______________________________________________

Theo states that being fearless doesn't mean eliminating fear. It means knowing how to leverage fear. To do that, you need to know a few things about what you are dealing with.

I asked my friend Jean Tien to share her thoughts on Fear as an Intuitive Mindset Coach.

*"Fear is nothing more than a hologram - it may look real,
and even sound real, but when you look at it closer,
you'll realize that there is no substance to it."*

*"That said, fear is not meant to be conquered or pushed away;
instead, it is still deserving of your attention
so that you can see how hollow your fear truly is
so that you can then dismiss the fear for good."*

***Jean Tien***

I still remember the night after my speech beating myself up for failing. It wasn't until I starting writing down my feelings that I was able to start to remove that fear.

# CHAPTER 3

# WHY DID I STRUGGLE WITH THAT SPEECH?

---

So, why in the moment did I struggle with that speech so much?

If you remember what we learned about how fear actually works, you can create a plan of attack to leave fear aside. Once fear is removed, confidence can take its rightful place.

Here is what I learned from my research on fear answered by some of my amazing friends...

## Fear is healthy and comes in many shades

I asked my friend Ashwini "Ash" Prasad to share her thoughts on Fear as an anti-racist educator, screenwriter, and her work leading with equity and justice.

*"Fear, when acknowledged, is healthy."*

*"I am uncertain if unacknowledged fear is healthy and an interesting thought question for a later time. In this moment, to realize we are fearful allows us the starting point to move forward in ways we cannot imagine."*

*"I truly believe we are scared of our power and how great we are; this recognition can debilitate some people and lead to incorrect self-characterizations such as, "impostor syndrome," as a result."*

*"The aforementioned is one example when fear is debilitating."*

*"The thing with fear, like the ego, is that fear can disguise itself as healthy and good. Some of us affirm in seemingly positive ways but the root of the affirmation is fear based. For example, people will say, "it is what it is," and stay here."*

*"While accepting a situation and your reaction is important, simply accepting a situation is rooted in fear because you're not looking at how to change the situation in the future or reflecting on how to avoid the situation."*

*"The fear manifestation, the shade, is in the passive acceptance rather than proactive thoughts and actions. Fear is healthy, comes in many shades, and our volition to move past fear is where new opportunities and human resilience lie."*

***Ashwini Prasad***

1. **Fear is not as automatic as you think**

Hear the words of my friend Beth as she discusses Fear and how we all have someone in our corner.

*"I believe fear is an intrinsic human reaction that was built into us to protect us. We must work through our irrational thoughts by taking small steps to overcome fears that do not serve us."*

*"When we overcome fears, they won't automatically show up."*

*"I believe God gives us power over fear when we believe in Him and His love for us. Knowing He has only my best planned, I trust that through all circumstances I am becoming more the person He wants me to be."*

***Beth Crosby***

Certain situations can cause us fear when we are uncertain of our talents and abilities to execute. I would have rather gotten into the ring with Mike Tyson than deliver that speech again, why?

I know what is going to happen when I get into the ring with Mike. I'm going to get hit and then get knocked out and then collect a nice check. But not knowing if you are going to screw up is more nerve-racking then knowing the outcome.

2. **You don't need to be in danger to be scared and the more scared you feel, the scarier things will seem**

Christopher and Gary share how they suggest battling Fear.

*"It's a state of mind being present to offset fear. Life and death situations will trigger fear to feel scared. We do not have to allow feeling scared to hold us back in situations that are not life threatening. Be present and calm is key."*

*"Be present often to offset fear and with clarity anything is possible."*

*"Give without expectation and receive without resistance"*

***Christopher Salem***

*"Many things in life are scary – some terrifying, paralyzing. Fear can make you quit before you start. If you only do the things that don't scare you, or wait until they don't scare you, some things you'll never even try.*

*So, you must act. Be scared. Do brave"*

***Gary J. Lanham***

Anticipating Fear can be more frightful then the act the we are afraid of. So, are there actions we can take to overcome this?

3. **Fear dictates the actions you take**

Empowering purpose driven minds to turn traumas into triumphs through holistic living, my friend Hilary shares her thoughts on Fear and the actions to take.

*"Fear only dictates the actions you take if you give fear permission to take action."*

*"That's the beauty of life... you have a choice. Our **Amygdala** (a collection of nuclei found deep within the temporal lobe involved with the experience of emotions) loves to go to fight or flight mode. That's just neuroscience. And since fear is part instinct, part learned, and part taught, it's a normal feeling that, when we are aware of it, we can have it work for us rather than against us."*

*"As soon as we realize we already have the tools to alter our thoughts, moods and behaviors and live powerfully, we can make empowering choices that allow us to be kind to the mind and be guided differently."*

***Hilary Russo***

4. **The more real the threat, the more heroic your actions**

With an overpowering passion to help youth in mentorship roles Phillip shares some of how he has his clients battle Fear.

*"Part of the reason most remain in a frustrated state in their life is a refusal to embrace the threats that come with pursuing greater."*

*"Instead of embracing the criticism and pain that comes with pursuing success, most shy away from the heroic actions, courage or bravery needed to "save the day" or translated personally, "save their own life."*

*"Big goal or dream means the more heroic actions required."*

***Phillip Yacinthe***

Remember our experience with Mr. T-Rex?

When the situation arrives us humans can do amazing things to help someone trapped under a car or even run super-fast to get away from Mr. T-Rex. How can we learn to harness this Fear to help us with Fear and Confidence?

When we go to war with fear in our own lives, it's good to have a battle plan in mind. From my own experience, I've outlined one that I think might help.

First things First.... You have to take a "Time- Out"

- Try physically removing yourself from the situation for at least 30 min by doing something you enjoy; it this is possible. (For me it would be going to the gym or listening to some 80's Heavy Metal.)
- Put a smile on your face by attempting to do something for someone else.
- Find an excuse to slip away and have a few minutes of peace and quiet.

Let's now discuss some of the actions we can take to help us relax and begin to lesson that Fear and start to build Confidence.

## Practice deep breathing

My friend Judy shares her tips on dealing with the feeling of Fear.

*"Faith over fear."*

*"Fear is formative, and we should use it to fuel our passion."*

*"Take deep breaths, get really still, and focus on your breathing."*

*"Breathe in for three and exhale for three. As you breathe out, imagine that you are breathing out fear, worry, and anxiety. As you breathe in, imagine that you are breathing in confidence, peace, and calm."*

*"Every time you feel the fear and anxiety coming on, get still, and focus on your breathing. This is an exercise that you can do anywhere. Keep the faith; you got this. You are more than enough."*

***"Remember always that you are Badass."***

***Judy McCutcheon***

This is why meditation works for so many people. Meditation is the process of training your mind to focus and redirect your thoughts.

Its benefits can be: Reducing Stress, Reduce Anxiety, Promote Emotional Well-being, Enhance Self-Awareness, Increase

Attention Span, Reduce Memory Loss, Increase Kindness, Fight Addictions, improve a Good Night's Sleep, Help Decrease Pain, Reduce Blood Pressure, you can Practice it Anywhere.

I highly recommend visiting **Chopra.com** to learn more about Meditation.

## Listen to some music

Music can have a profound effect on both the emotions and the body.

Faster music can make you feel more alert and concentrate better.

Music is effective for relaxation and stress management.

Music can connect us with the automatic nervous system or brain function, heartbeat, and blood pressure all tied to the limbic system.

This is the place that your emotions and feelings live.

## So, what type of music reduces stress the best?

Native American, Celtic, Indian stringed-instruments, drums, and flutes are very effective at relaxing the mind even when played moderately loud.

Natural sounds like wind and rain can help as well.

Endorphins are released from your body when you play an instrument or sing. I guarantee you that I have a lot of endorphins in my car from all that singing I do while driving.

Mornings are some of the best times to listen to music. It can ease your nerves and even increase your confidence when getting ready to present in that business meeting.

Add more music to your life and sing a little bit more in the shower or in the car. I know when I sing I smile. When I smile I'm more relaxed.

## Chillax...Have a cup of tea

The simple act of taking a moment to prepare a cup of tea and slow down can help to relieve stress and leave you feeling a little more balanced. Ritualized relaxation is one of the many benefits of tea.

The type of tea you choose to brew can also help to soothe stress and anxiety. One of the key reason's tea is so beneficial for your health is due to L-Theanine, an amino acid that helps to balance mood. Although theanine levels differ because of many different factors, teas also contain a number of beneficial ingredients that can help to settle your mind and reduce stress on your body.

**CHAMOMILE TEA**: This tea helps to naturally increase serotonin and melatonin levels in your body, leaving you feeling relaxed without feeling drowsy. Plus, it can help relieve tension by soothing muscle aches and headaches often associated with stress and anxiety.

**PEPPERMINT TEA:** Because it helps to relax muscles, peppermint tea can also help soothe tension headaches brought on by stress and anxiety, even just by inhaling the scent of a warm mug of peppermint tea. Plus, if you're feeling anxious and overwhelmed by all you have to get done, peppermint tea can be a great option to give you a natural energy boost while also leaving you feeling calm and balanced.

If you would like to see all of the Eight Best Teas for Stress & Anxiety and all of their tea related products please visit **Sips by** at **https://www.sipsby.com/blogs/functional-herb-spotlights/best-teas-for-stress-anxiety**

## Go get some fresh air

I couldn't think of anyone better to share their thoughts on how exercise and living a healthy life can help you battle Fear and keep it from entering your life then my friend Bruno the best Trainer and Fitness Coach I know.

*"Now more than ever it's important to get out of your house. Get out of your work space and experience the outdoors. The air and the sun are slowly beginning to no longer be in our lives due to COVID and the ability to stay inside at all times."*

*"And it's more important than ever to appreciate and be grateful for seemingly small things like getting outside for fresh air."*

***Doc Bruno Gervasi***

## Work out

*"If you're not working out right now,*
*you're leaving so much off the table in your ability to be successful"*

*"Every uber successful person makes sure their physical self is in tip top shape because they understand that the better, they take care of themselves physically the stronger and more fit they'll be in every area of their life."*

*"Their mental performance, the emotional strength to name a few."*

***Doc Bruno Gervasi***

For me there is nothing more relaxing then a great workout. Working out at the gym allows me to spend some quiet time with my own thoughts similar to meditation for others.

Getting the heart pounding and the blood flowing throughout the body allows me to conquer my day when I work out in the morning.

Our body and mind are truly one in the same and we must take care of both to have a successful and long and healthy life.

## Find gratitude

Sometimes you get to meet your social media connections in person. These can then turn into true friendships that can last a lifetime. My LinkedIn friend Victor and I had that opportunity to meet in person in 2019 and here he shares these touching thoughts on finding gratitude.

*"When my daughter was facing a life-threatening disease and there were many negative days in a row it made me feel discouraged and fearful."*

*"It got to a point where all I could focus on was the high probability of a negative outcome. I became determined to change my mindset and did so by publicly announcing one a day what I was grateful for."*

*"As I did this, with each day I started to experience less fear and began to see possibilities where I did not before."*

*"In short, expressing gratitude gave me a spirit and mindset of hope. "It was a game changer for me."*

***Victor Hallock***

If my friend Victor can find hope while expressing gratitude during a very difficult time in his life so can you. Here are a few ways you can practice gratitude in your own life:

- Keep a gratitude journal
- Write a positive review for a business
- Write thank you notes
- Meditate/reflect on what you are grateful for in your life

## Embrace what you can and cannot control

My friends Remo, Bruno, and Corrie now will share their thoughts on how to embrace what you can and what you cannot control.

*"Fear helps you judge things right or wrong*
*but when fear is invoked forcibly by an external source*
*the outcome can be unpredictably dangerous."*

***Remo Chhetri***

*"There's so much we cannot control. And the better you can look at those things in your control and dominate them with all of your will the better you're going to feel*
*and the more successful you'll be!"*

***Doc Bruno Gervasi***

*"In my experience... fear is directly related to confidence, as well as feelings of control. In general, the more confident people are the more in control they feel so fear isn't as much of a challenge."*

*"Unfortunately, the only person who can help someone become more confident is oneself. It requires action in doing whatever task is driving that fear until the point that they feel comfortable enough to no longer fear it."*

***Corrie LoGiudice***

## Spend time with a pet

The love of a pet can have so many therapeutic benefits to our everyday lives and our emotional well-being.

*"Dogs elicit a hormone referred to as Oxytocin. Other pets do as well. Cats, horses—almost any type of pet helps people manage fear, loneliness, and anxiety."*

*"Certified therapy dogs are specifically trained to help those dealing with the effects of PTSD. This is the core of the definition of the human-animal bond."*

***Lesley Osborn***

There is nothing better than the love of a pet. And for me it's the love of our special new addition to our family, Koa, our French Bulldog.

They look at us with those cute eyes and want to do nothing more than to please us.

I know when I have had a hard day spending some time with my dog will allow me to forget about my human world for a moment and just share all of that love and feeling of true happiness.

1. **You have to own it and don't fight the Fear or anxiety**

It's not just going to go away but guess what? You are still alive and the sun will still come up tomorrow. Let's face it we are our own worst enemy. So, accept that it happened and soak it all in, until it leaves and rest assured that the more you fail or have fear the easier it will get.

- **Embrace those emotions.**
- **Acknowledge irrational beliefs about your failure.**
- **Accept that it did happen and own it.**
- **Ask yourself what you learned from this situation...find the positive.**
- **Create a plan....and that is just what you are going to do.**

2. **Find a quiet place after steps 1 and 2**

You need to start writing down the experience. It will help you move through it by sharing it with yourself.

You don't need to share it with anyone else. But the action of writing down your experience will allow you to accept it and move on faster. When it happens again and rest assured it will you will accept it and move on quicker.

I have never journaled my thoughts ever, at least not until that Oct 21$^{st}$ 2020 plane flight home from Orlando. I can't believe how therapeutic it was. Writing it all down allowed me to move on from it faster and accept it more easily. This journaling thing may have some legs.

Give yourself hours and hours to start writing that experience, every difficult word, because as you write down everything that happened it will hurt less.

Now we would be kidding ourselves if we thought it was just going to go away after a few hours writing down your experience but, for some reason writing down what happened allows you to accept it and that's right, move on quicker.

3. **Now go and reward yourself for having Fear**

Yes, treat yourself to an amazing meal, massage, a walk in the park, go shopping and spend some good alone time. Embrace what went right because I know that something did in fact go right.

I learned a lot from that speaking engagement. People connected with me afterwards and asked questions of me. I even got a new client because of it.

We are so hard on ourselves. We are often our own worst critics.

Maybe, just maybe, we suffer from something other than just fear.

Buckle up, because now I get to discuss something worse than fear? ...is this even possible?

Yes, it is possible, this heinous condition's name is "Impostor Syndrome".

# CHAPTER 4

# WHAT THE HECK IS THIS IMPOSTOR SYNDROME THING?

Wikipedia defines Impostor Syndrome as the following:

**Impostor syndrome** (also known as **impostor phenomenon**, **impostorism**, **fraud syndrome** or the **impostor experience**) is a psychological pattern in which an individual doubts their skills, talents or accomplishments and has a persistent internalized fear of being exposed as a "fraud".

Despite external evidence of their competence, those experiencing this phenomenon remain convinced that they are frauds, and do not deserve all they have achieved.

Individuals with impostorism incorrectly attribute their success to luck, or interpret it as a result of deceiving others into thinking they are more intelligent than they perceive themselves to be.

While early research focused on the prevalence among high-achieving women, impostor syndrome has been recognized to affect both men and women equally.

If you have spent any time with me or if you know me on LinkedIn, I always have a smile on my face.

All of my former bosses, you know when I worked for "the man"; always said they appreciated the fact that I never dwell on yesterday's results and numbers whether they were good or bad. I believe this is just one of the many things that made me a great leader of others.

If my teams had a bad day, week or month we ever-so-briefly discussed it, never to bring it up again because you can only gain knowledge from yesterday's results. Now yes you can implement improvements to allow you to possibly learn from those mistakes; But you cannot directly impact yesterday. Move on with a focus on what you can control and influence. Those are the actions you take today and the attitude you accept.

Leadership along with positivity is infectious; If you mope around about the results from yesterday, you will, in fact, effect today. But not with the results or attitude you want to convey.

So, I guess you can say Leaders show confidence and the lack of fear; At the least they may never let you know they have it because leaders take on the problems and issues to serve their teams. We all know you can't successfully lead long term with fear at the forefront.

I guess it would be prudent to tell you that prior to leaving my 9 to 5 job in December of 2019 I had suffered from "Impostor Syndrome" for months prior.

Now you may be saying what is that made up word you are talking about? Well, it actually is a real thing and something that I suffered from.

Don't worry it's not contagious but you can be affected by it, so let me explain how I was inflicted.

It was around September of 2019 and my side hustle of writing resumes, while working my 9 to 5 job, was steadily increasing.

I still didn't think I could do this full time because I had yet to truly believe in my newly acquired skills.

When we gain a new skill, it can be hard for us to allow ourselves to say we are good at it let alone great at it, why?

A newly gained skill or knowledge is just that, still new. Normally we have not gained the confidence to allow ourselves to say we are amazing at it, yet others are seeing us as an "in-fact" SME (subject – matter – expert).

We are our own worst critics. Why is that? I truly believe it's because we don't want to seem too confident or maybe we fear it comes across as arrogant. Who likes those people, right?

So, we keep it inside. Even though people were coming to me on LinkedIn, -when my entire LinkedIn profile screamed what I did in my 9 to 5 job and nowhere on my LinkedIn profile did it say anything about writing resumes or providing LinkedIn advice-people were still messaging me and saying, "Hey will you look at my resume and provide some advice?" Or, "How much will you charge me to write my resume because I want to hire you".

Even with people coming to me after seeing a recent LinkedIn video post of mine where I shared some resume tips, or LinkedIn guidance, I still didn't make the connection, why? Impostor Syndrome strikes again!

I was diagnosed with a genuine, confirmed case of it by multiple LinkedIn doctors', three of my close LinkedIn influencer friends; Cory Warfield, Anthony English, Joe Apfelbaum.

Each of them told me why I had it and told me how I could get rid of it. They said it was very easy to put into remission. I'm only too happy to share their prescription, for those who feel themselves coming down with a case.

They all three told me, -on three separate calls, all within three weeks' time; that if others see me as an expert then guess what? That means, I'm an expert.

But I still said to them, well I know I'm an expert in my 9 to 5 job because I had been in that industry for over 18+ years.... but I still don't understand how I can be seen as an expert at something I hadn't really been doing too long.

All of my LinkedIn "doctors" agreed that it had nothing to do with me, but how others saw me. If you provide value and can obviously help others then you have the right to accept the fact that you are an expert and should allow others that perception of you. WOW!!!

Those are the words I needed to hear.

If others saw me as an expert, -because what is an expert but someone that provides knowledge and skills/value in a particular area to others, then heck, who am I to say anything different?

I was cured just like that! Well, it might have taken about another three weeks of continuing to remind myself that I am what others see me as.

Now I go back to that speech as I'm typing this out and realize something.

Because it was my first paid speaking engagement, I didn't allow myself to be seen as a subject matter expert because I had never done it before.

But my friend Mark believed in me, the person who referred me to the organization that hired me. And I'm sure the organization that hired me spied on my LinkedIn profile and took a look at my work and was convinced I was an SME.

So, now I know what truly caused me to screw up during the first five minutes of my speech. I didn't allow myself to have the true confidence to say I was a subject matter expert at speaking only because I had never been paid to do it prior.

I'm sure I will crush the next one. Oh yes, there will be a next one. I had suffered from Impostor Syndrome once again, but this time for a different skill.

That darn Impostor Syndrome can rear its ugly head from time to time. It is what we do when we acknowledge it -when it is happening to us that's most important.

So maybe confidence or the lack there of is part of the reason Impostor Syndrome even exists in the first place. That's a very interesting thought.

Life lessons are not always easy but unfortunately necessary to both learn and grow.

I believe my friend Joe Apfelbaum sums up Fear and Impostor Syndrome quite brilliantly by sharing his thoughts here. Please consider following Joe and my other friends on LinkedIn.

*"Are you afraid that people will find out who you really are?"*

*"Deep down we all have a feeling that we are not enough."*

*"A fear that if someone found out our secret, they too would see that as the truth and we would suffer shame for being an imposter."*

*"This fear is impostor syndrome."*

*"I have talked to many CEOs that have grown very large businesses and no matter how much success they have, this fear is still present for them."*

*"How does one have more confidence to be able to keep taking action even in spite of this fear."*

*"For me, I use courage to take action. Courage is the spark inside you that helps you take action even though you know good and well you might not be worthy. If you did not have FEAR you would not need to have courage."*

*"Courage is being able to take action, in spite of fear."*

*"You might have FEAR that you will not be love, fear that you will fail or you might have fear that you might succeed and it still won't make you feel fulfilled so you end up sabotaging yourself subconsciously."*

*"Regardless, you have the ability to still take action. You have the ability to commit and not quit."*

*"You have the ability to live your values, make a difference that you know is true and keep moving forward."*

*"Fear is just a FEELING, a feeling that comes and goes depending on the story that you believe in the moment. Action is what cures that fear. Once you take action, you feel that rush inside that just*

*takes over and when you GET IN THE ZONE from taking action and stopping all the thoughts, you know what it means to be alive."*

*"That is why they say that self-expression is life."*

*"It takes courage to put yourself out there. It takes courage to TRUST that even if you feel like you are not enough, you ARE enough."*

*"Fear is false evidence that appears real. That means that the PROOF that you have that you are not worthy of success or not worthy of love is a LIE."*

*"You are brilliant, wonderful, amazing, incredible and worthy. You, the way you are right now, with all your weaknesses, flaws, imperfections and any excuses and failures are PERFECT."*

*"That's what makes you human. The ability to BE with all those things that we are not complete with. You are a human BEING and you are loved." The best way to inspire self-confidence, is to experience self-love."*

*"The best way to get everyone else to trust in you, is for you to trust yourself."*

*"The fastest way to overcome your fears of not being enough is to SEE that you are enough exactly the way you are."*

*"Impostor Syndrome will come knocking at your door and you will be home with a smile and give it a hug, because no one can take loving yourself away from you."*

***Joe Apfelbaum***

---

So, now we know what Impostor Syndrome is and some steps we can take to overcome it. Sharing my experience and writing it all down has been very therapeutic.

So, why does journaling work and how can we expand our knowledge on the subject?

# CHAPTER 5

## The Neuroscience of Journaling

I could share my thoughts on Journaling but I thought I would save it for the professionals. My friend Heather is an expert on all things Journaling.

So, please now read as my friend Heather Pickens shares her expertise and thoughts on the benefits of Journaling and the How's and Why's behind it.

*"Our brains have become slower due to the daily repetition and time spent being glued to our digital devices and researchers have coined the phrase,* ***"digital dementia."***

*"This digital landscape has also created a huge mental health surge that has contributed to the collective fear, lack of focus and lower confidence levels. Journaling has been proven through science-based research to be a powerful tool in counterbalancing these issues."*

*"Journaling helps the brain to go analog and can be used to reflect on your day, which is an ancient Stocic practice. The more you focus on reflection and what you can change the more confidence you can build within. Imagine yourself as a scientist of your own mind."*

*"It's important to be a collector of data to gain insight on your day so you can focus on building a growth mindset. Journaling can be used*

*to create a mental script so that you can change that internal narrative from* ***"I am not good enough to I am a powerful leader****!"*

*"The repetition of journaling changes the brain's neuroplasticity, which can transform those fear-based programs almost instantly."*

*"For example, if you have a meeting or sales call that you dread, you can create a mental script to calm down your nervous system to focus on future outcomes. This type of training is similar to what Olympic Athletes have used to win Gold medals."*

*"Your nervous system is responsible for activating a fight or flight response or feeling like a Zen Master. The more you reinforce building these connections using journaling the more powerful you will become."*

*"Another benefit of journaling is learning how to organize your thoughts.* ***The Vision Method*** *utilizes a framework that teaches you how to think so you can organize every area of your demanding life."*

*"Having an organizational framework balances the nervous system and switches off the mind chatter of your high achiever's mindset while increasing confidence levels to master your day."*

***Heather Pickens***

Sounds like I was not giving the act of journaling its credit prior to writing this book. I have found the ability to let go of that Impostor Syndrome by writing down my thoughts I was having about my dreaded speaking engagement. I have included Heather's contact info in the back of the book should you want to learn more about journaling.

# CHAPTER 6

# CONFIDENCE

---

I think you and I have found the connection. We've broken the secret code that's kept so many so locked up for so long.

I can't believe it took us so long to make the connection between the lack of fear and true confidence.

So, what is true confidence?

Now we know what fear can do and we now can take the necessary steps to leave fear aside. How do we gain confidence? Or, will the lack of fear turn into confidence?

In an article simply called "Confidence" from GoodTherapy® shares the following:

---

**WHAT IS CONFIDENCE?**

Confidence can occur as a one-time feeling.

Prior to giving that speech I felt confident that it would go well because I had rehearsed it for weeks and crushed it the night before.

People with high self-confidence will feel comfortable believing others like them, that they can perform well at work, and that they can meet the daily demands of life.

**Confidence** is a person's belief that a chosen course of action is the right choice and that they can properly perform that action. As a personality trait, confidence is sometimes referred to as self-confidence.

People who have high levels of self-confidence may feel sure they will achieve what they set out to do and maintain a steady sense of control over the outcomes in their lives.

Self-confident people generally trust in their abilities, their influence, and their decisions.

They may feel comfortable in their ability to perform well in a variety of life tasks and experience less anxiety and self-doubt than people with low self-confidence.

**Self-esteem and well-being:** Self-confidence can inform how people feel about themselves in a recurring way. In other words, the more self-confident people feel, the more likely they will be to take risks to improve their situations. The more risks they take, the greater the likelihood they will find success.

Now I know with potential risks comes the potential of fear entering our minds thus creating the opportunity for us to have anxiety take hold and then yes, the potential risk of failure.

*"Confidence in one can make him/her fly over greater obstacles when the entire world chases that particular person in order to pull them down and clip off their wings."*

***Remo Chhetri***

**Empowerment:** Self-confidence can impact a person's sense of self-efficacy.

The more a person believes in one's self, the more empowered that person is likely to feel, especially with regard to trying new things. Self-confidence can also have a snowball effect on a person's ability to achieve personal and professional goals.

Thus, leaving Impostor Syndrome left behind to never rear its ugly head.

*"Fear can be a driver, and confidence can be an obstacle – it's all about expectation and energy."*

*"I often say that 'Perfection is the enemy of progress'*
*but to take it a layer deeper:*
*Fear of being imperfect often causes individuals*
*to keep their genius hidden,*
*but in truth all masterpieces can be constructed to be flawed,*
*and this inherently is what draws such adoration."*

***Cory Warfield***

**Anxiety reduction:** A self-confident attitude can help people feel better able to overcome obstacles. As a result, they may experience less ambiguity when facing new challenges and less fear and anxiety associated with unfamiliar situations.

They say attitude is everything and whoever "they" are they are 100% correct.

Attitude is an all-encompassing term that defines your outlook and approach to any situation in life. It also includes your inner thoughts and outward expressions.

In the end, attitude determines everything you say and everything you do....and now fear will not stand a chance against you because you know fears limited ability against your new confidence.

**Less stress, more energy:** People who are self-confident may be less likely to experience anxiety and self-doubt about their goals and actions and may accordingly experience less stress.

Sky's the limit when you have less stress and increased energy.... think of all of those entrepreneurs that exude confidence.

Being confident in one's decisions without worrying about the outcome is what successful entrepreneurs do. They are more worried about moving quickly to implement then worrying about if it works out.

*"Real Confidence is always earned through hard work. So, work hard and master your craft; whatever that may be and the confidence will come."*

*"The phrase I don't care what others think isn't confidence its arrogance or ignorance."*

*"If you want "Real Confidence" know your mental. Do tough things; go through hell and never quit. When you come out on the other side you will be better and know it. We are molded in the toughest of times not when it's easy."*

***Josh Cole***

**Better interpersonal relationships:** If self-confidence promotes happiness, then it follows that it can improve the quality of a person's relationships. Because people who experience self-confidence tend to trust in themselves and their abilities, they may feel empowered and be more successful than those who lack self-confidence.

A better interpersonal relationship is a quick cure from Impostor Syndrome.

*"Without balance it is impossible to focus on what matters to you, to be secure in yourself, to build the life you want, and to have fun doing it."*

***Theo Tsaousides, Ph.D.***

**Success:** A typical human goal is achieving success. The more people achieve, the more skilled they may become.

The Great One.... Wayne Gretzky said:

*"You miss 100% of the shots you don't take."*

Don't ever pass up an opportunity to fail.... Yes, fail.

When you pass an opportunity to fail.... you pass up on an opportunity to **Win!**

*"You either learn the way or you learn that you don't have the answer. So, you either move on alone or solicit help."*

***"But never quit."***

*"Either lose or learn; the choice is yours.*
*Choose to learn or losing will stay with you."*

***Josh Cole***

Your plan of attack to battle fear worked. We identified the fear, we learned how and what tools to use to battle fear and then you came up with a plan! Awesome job! Oh, we haven't put a plan together yet?

By sharing your experience, you have already put the steps in motion to start your plan to battle Fear. Discussing Confidence can help ensure the success of your plan that I will help you put together at the end of this book.

I think you know what steps we are going to implement now and if you said: "We are going to describe each of the steps to implement and gain confidence and then expand on each of them individually and come up with an exercise on what you can do to remove fear" ....... WOW!!

You either must be a mind reader or you are the person sitting next to me on the airplane watching me write this. That's just a very weird coincidence. Either way you are 100% correct.

Here is what we learned from our research on confidence.

1. Confidence is a belief and not something that happens. Confidence takes time to gain and that is where Fear can enter.

During those times of self-doubt watch out, because here comes Fear around the corner.

2. Self-esteem is developed over time. I want you to say to yourself right now, *"I'm great at...*

Insert a talent or something you have been recently developing:

3. Repeat step 2 each and every day after you wake up because you need to start believing it and hearing it.

Say it in your mirror, yes this is silly and some of you may even think it's dumb. It is silly, but you need to see someone saying you are great at it. I can't think of a single person more perfect than you to tell yourself how great you are.

*"I don't think saying positive things over and over again can make me a positive person. I was created to be a positive person and so I just need to act like it!"*

*"I do need to choose my attitude and control my thoughts. When negativity rears its head, I simply focus on things like,* ***"I can do all things through Christ who gives me strength."*** *or I decide to give to others."*

*"When I give to others, I take my eyes off of whatever negatives are happening to me. How can anyone feel negative when they are sincerely helping someone else?"*

***Gene Girdley***

4. Overcoming obstacles at work is easy. Why? Because you do it each and every day. You know how to do your job even if something comes at you from out of the blue.

Anxiety only rears its ugly head when we don't know what to do and we are not confident that we can do it.

Fear will never enter our minds if we have confidence in our back pocket.

*"Fear and Confidence are closely tied to experience. Nike says, "Just do it!" The only way to walk is to take a step. The only way to swim is to get in the water."*

*"To overcome fear, and to build confidence. You have to act. You will fail, but you will learn how to compensate and improve each time you try."*

***Gene Girdley***

5. Never worry about the outcome of anything. You have no control over what others will do or think, you can only control your own thoughts and emotions.

I want you to care less about the outcome and care more about sharing your thoughts.

The rest is up to the person receiving your message, your work proposal, your speech, etc.

Let's circle back to that man pushing up that rock up the hill on the cover of my book.

Now imagine if that rock was Confidence and every time you got close to the top of the hill you had that Confidence pushed back down deep inside you to never rise to the top.

I will share this story of this man and the rock with you soon but what I want you to realize is we can burden ourselves with so many things in our lives. Gaining the strength to push up that rock is key and I'm not talking about physical strength.

Mental strength can move mountains, or the lack of it can keep us from even starting our journey up that infinite, never ending hill.

Here are some thoughts and insights into the steps you must take to gain true confidence, or hold onto it once you developed it. The advice comes from some amazing thought leaders and friends.

## Block negative thoughts

*"Surround yourself with people that know you and ask for feedback. If they have positive things to say, then maybe the negative thoughts aren't really an accurate representation of you."*

***Jonaed Iqbal***

## Assertiveness training

*"Start small. Assert yourself in small situations where the consequences don't matter much. Normally when you would stay quiet at the store, just say something. Stand up for others."*

*"As you get practice, you will be more confident asserting yourself when it does matter."*

***Jonaed Iqbal***

## Build self-esteem

*"Build it one brick at a time."*

*"Your self-esteem may not be an accurate representation of you."*

*"It's okay to think you are good at things if you are actually good at them."*

*"Ask the people around you for feedback and what they think of you."*

***Jonaed Iqbal***

## Positive affirmations

*"Positive affirmations... I believe in truth over affirmations. What is true of me is that I'm created in God's image. I reflect His nature and He loves me for who I am. Because I believe that, I can live a life of positivity. What others think of me pales in comparison to who God says I am..."*

*"Fearfully and wonderfully made"*

*"Beloved"*

*"Cherished"*

*"A Pearl of Great Price"*

***Gene Girdley***

## Goal-setting and rewards

*"There has to be a benefit to any action. We don't set a goal just to set it. We desire to achieve because of what we will get when we arrive at the destination. The "prize" helps us keep going when the road is rough."*

***Gene Girdley***

My friend Anthony helped me shake that Impostor Syndrome during my very first battle with Fear and Confidence. So, I couldn't think of anyone better to share his detailed thoughts on the subject.

*"You're not the audience. You think you're not good enough. That you don't have confidence. And all the advice you get to believe in yourself, or "just do it!" ...well. That advice just doesn't do it for you."*

*"Want to know why?"*

*"Imagine you're an actor, or a singer about to walk out on stage."*

*"The audience is waiting. Your time is now."*

*"But you stay backstage. You won't go out there."*

*"Even with a crowd who are eager to see you, to hear you."*

*"They want you to do well. (That's what they paid for!)"*

*"But you hold back, because you're not good enough."*

*"You don't feel confident."*

*"You're a perfectionist."*

*"You know the pattern. You have the playbook. You are setting yourself up to beat yourself up."*

*"Can I remind you of one little thing?"*

*"You're not the audience. It's up to them to decide whether you're good enough, and they will be kinder to you than you are to yourself."*

*"You don't feel confident? Maybe you don't have to feel confident."*

*"You're already playing your role, and if you don't do it, nobody else will."*

*"You have no understudy."*

*"You have to do what only you can do."*

*"The audience will do their part, but only if you do yours."*

---

*"Some of them won't like your work. Never mind. They're not your real audience. Let them move on. Don't waste your time defending yourself."*

*"Some of them will think you're brilliant, even if, in your own mind, you knew it could have been better."*

*"Don't waste your time correcting their judgment or dismissing their appreciation."*

*"And some of them, the majority, will be grateful and kind and be glad that you could do what they would never do: step out on that stage."*

*"They will judge you as kindly as you would judge someone else who didn't feel confident."*

*"You've got enough of a job doing the work of the actor, the singer, the helper."*

*"You don't have the luxury of being the audience for your own play."*

*"And you definitely don't make a good critic".*

*"Leave that to others. You just play your part."*

*"Now, step out on the stage. It's your cue. Right now."*

*"They're waiting for you."*

***Anthony English***

# CHAPTER 7

# MY STORY

---

Writing this was very therapeutic because it allowed me to search out the "whys" behind Fear and gaining Confidence.

It allowed me to gain a better perspective about myself. Even as I was writing it helped me conquer my fears and gain increased confidence. I hope sharing it will bring others the relief from living with their own fear, no matter how small.

I just realized I haven't shared with you what I do for a living and you may be surprised to know that I'm a social media influencer on the LinkedIn platform.

---

## Sharing my LinkedIn journey with you...

The most amazing thing about finding out what you have become truly passionate about is sharing it with others.

Through my previous day job and now on the social media platform of LinkedIn, I've discovered a passion for continual learning and sharing with others what I've learned.

I started off searching for a new career and of course learning all of the wrong things to do along the way. By trial & error and from many amazingly giving LinkedIn members, I finally found the correct way to use LinkedIn.

I was surprised that during this time of being active I grew my following and connections very quickly. I stayed up late at night after a hard day's work to share and learn. I also got up early every morning to comment/post and ask a lot of questions of people I once called "Influencers".

As I was learning, I was posting content and commenting on relevant and interesting content. By doing this I continued to learn and meet so many amazing people along the way.

As my knowledge of how to navigate LinkedIn grew, I made sure to share this knowledge with others.

What I didn't realize early in my LinkedIn development was that I was in the beginning stages of finding my true passion.

This new interesting platform became a way for me to continue what I have always tried to be, which is a Servant Leader.

With my 9 to 5 career I have always been considered a good leader and developer of others. I always took pride in putting others first to get the results we needed to succeed in the business world.

My new interaction with LinkedIn allowed me to potentially influence even more people than what I was use to with my previous career.

LinkedIn provided me a platform for helping endless amounts of people.

How did I know this? I was seeing it happen daily.

I saw the amazing Oleg Vishnepolsky giving advice and commenting and connecting with others. Putting others first. This was jaw dropping for me.

I could not believe the selfless acts I was witnessing.

It was January 24$^{th}$ 2019 when I posted my first video on LinkedIn. How do I remember this day so vividly you ask?

I was sitting in the parking lot of my Kennewick store and it was my 50$^{th}$ birthday. Thank you for the birthday wishes.

I wanted to post a video on LinkedIn so I posted why I was so excited to turn 50. I explained that when you turn 50 you can contribute more to your 401k and I was ready to max that out so I shared it to the world.

World, might be too ambitious because I didn't have all that many followers at the time. Here is what I learned from posting that video, I learned that not everyone knew the info I was providing. I learned all you have to do on LinkedIn is share things you know, and FYI I am not a financial expert I just have some knowledge and interest on the subject of saving money.

I discovered that I didn't have to have a huge network to make a difference. I learned that we all can share and learn from one another here on LinkedIn and I was hooked.

It was about this same time the business owner I was working for was actively looking to sell the company. We were franchising stores left and right so I thought that maybe LinkedIn could help me land that new career.

I started reaching out to recruiters on LinkedIn and learned quickly that they do not reply on LinkedIn. I did have one recruiter reach out to me and tell me that what I was doing was not a best practice because most recruiters get hit up by unemployed people all the time. They just do not have the time to go through those additional emails.

So, I did some digging and came up with a great technique that I teach my clients today. When you see that job, you want to apply for, before applying reach out to others actually working at that same company, in the same position that you want to apply for.

I learned of a job at our Amazon call center here in town. I messaged a few people that worked at Amazon in that same role and guess what, one of them actually replied. We messaged back and forth and then met at Starbucks for coffee.

We discussed our similar careers, he worked for Teavana (Starbucks owned company) and I had previously worked at Starbucks myself. We discussed our management styles and then he told me he would contact me if a new position where to open that he thought I might be a great fit for.

A few weeks later I got a message that a new position had opened and he put me in for a referral and I landed the interview. My new connection had come through.

I ended up getting multiple interviews, but I did not get the job and that was ok.

I learned an important lesson. You can leverage your network on LinkedIn to land interviews and potentially new careers that you might otherwise not know about. I shared this knowledge with anyone and everyone that would listen to me.

Then an amazing person by the name of Cory Warfield connected with me on LinkedIn. I was thinking, why is this "Influencer" wanting to connect with me? Why would someone as busy as Cory want to connect with little ole me?

I commented on a few of his posts and then one day Cory said, "Let's connect". We had already connected on LinkedIn so I had no idea what Cory meant, until he invited me to get on a call together! I couldn't believe my simple strategy was paying off so well!

I'm still trying to understand why I took the call. I won't bore you with the details of the call but I will tell you one little blurb from our conversation.

I had just told Cory that I believe I was about to truly find out what I was passionate about, giving back to others. I told Cory I had recently volunteered at my local unemployment office providing resume and LinkedIn tips to their customers. It felt amazing to provide help to these people looking for new careers.

Then we discussed that job interview with Amazon. Cory said, "I'm happy you didn't get that job because from what you have told me you're going to do BIG things here soon enough."

Only weeks after that call with Cory I started providing resume service for free for just about anyone and everyone. I also started helping LinkedIn members with their LinkedIn profiles while continuing to grow my knowledge of the platform.

I provided my services for free for months because it was fun to provide help to others that seen me as a subject matter expert.

But I was not willing to accept money from anyone because you guessed it...I was suffering from Impostor Syndrome. I didn't know I was suffering because I didn't know I had it or even what it was.

It wasn't until a video conversation with Anthony English and then shortly after a phone call with Joe Apfelbaum, two people I looked up to at the time, and still do to this day, that I totally embraced the fact that you can be an expert at something you have not been doing all that long.

Those calls meant the world to me. Those calls allowed me to accept the fact that, if others see me as an expert, guess what? I must be an expert.

I've learned that it doesn't matter how long you been practicing a particular skill, what matters is whether others receive value from you. If they do guess what? Yes, you are in fact an expert.

You don't have the be the best to call yourself an expert. If that was the case there would be only one expert in every field! You would have to wait until that person died for the next person to step up to claim the crown of expert.

Once a accepted the fact that I provided real value I allowed myself to charge my clients.

I was having fun! I was still working my 9 to 5 job 55+ hours a week, working nights and weekends on resumes and having Zoom calls (before Zoom was a BIG thing) with my LinkedIn clients. I knew I couldn't do both forever but was having so much fun with my new side hustle.

So, I started working my side hustle more and more until I was totally confident that I could leave my current job and start my own business. After I had proved it to myself, I just had one more person to convince.

# CHAPTER 8

# MY STORY CONTINUED

We have to go back a little bit in time to April 26th 2012.

It's a day after my wedding to my wonderful bride Jennifer and I had a voice mail on my phone from my boss. Maybe it was congratulating me on my wedding, maybe something had happened to one of the stores I oversee??

So, I go to our hotel room and give him a call.

The news wasn't good. Our company had eliminated 70 District Managers and guess what! I was one of them. Now you may be thinking, what boss calls his employee and tells them on their honeymoon that their job was eliminated?

Well, to my bosses defense the company was going live to tell the entire company what had happened on Friday and he wanted me to know prior to hearing about it from someone else.

So, now I get to walk down to the beach where my bride of less than 24 hours is laying out basking in the Bahama's sun and tell her I lost my job.

I shared this story with you to tell you how amazing my wife is and how do I now, some 8 years later, convince her that I want to leave my day job and become self-employed.

My wife had been seeing the fun I was having with my side hustle and all this time had been seeing the success I was having. She had been seeing the extra money I was bringing in so convincing her to allow me to leave my job was easier but still not easy.

Going out on your own is never a sure thing. A lot can happen. But I knew if I could put in 50+ hours a week writing resumes and all of the other services I provided, I could achieve the goals I had set for myself.

So, on December 13th 2019 I left my day job and the rest is history.

Almost a year has passed and I don't regret a thing. I'm not one of those that says I wish I had done this years ago because I do truly believe we are a combination of all of our experiences and when the time is right, the time is right.

I have met so many amazing people on the LinkedIn platform that have allowed me to learn, share and laugh along the way. It's because of these relationships I have created, that I'm able to now do what I truly want to do.

You can find me on LinkedIn sharing videos on numerous topics but mostly resume advice and tips to how to build your online LinkedIn presence. I focused on teaching the average LinkedIn user and or job seeker how to properly build their professional brand. I showed them how to truly network on LinkedIn for those aggressively seeking that new career. In short, I provide value, whether they hire me, or not.

Now you may be saying how is someone that is extremely comfortable sharing videos of himself to sometimes hundreds of thousands of people, how did this individual choke during the beginning of his speech?

When you are attempting something new for the very first time you have the desire to get it right, right?

So, enter the nerves and butterfly's, that actually felt like bats, and I was toast.

I will tell you after the first 5 min of utter disgust with myself I then pulled it together and the rest of my speaking engagement was great. Okay, maybe good is a better term.

At the end of the day, I provided value. I know this because some of the attendees thanked me, connected with me on LinkedIn, maybe out of pity, but I truly believe it was because they saw the value in the rest of my speech.

With a current following of over 36,000+ on LinkedIn I'll be on the LinkedIn platform sharing daily resume, interview, and LinkedIn coaching tips as long as people take something away from it. I do it because I enjoy and really love helping others. The money? Well, let's say that's a nice bonus.

As my network continues to grow, I continue learning and sharing daily because I believe that a life where I get the privilege to both share and learn on a daily basis allows me to smile even less than 24 hours after that terrible beginning to that speech.

Therapy comes in many forms for people.

If you have surgery on a broken bone you normally have therapy to help you heal. Maybe you are entering therapy for a recent death of a loved one or a marriage you are attempting to salvage.

For me therapy came in the form of writing down my thoughts during my flight home after a difficult and yet surprisingly emotional experience. I know that I went through something amazing because I still have a huge smile on while typing away at the keyboard.

Sure, I might be a little nervous during my next paid speaking engagement, but there will be another, because when we go through something in life, we learn from it, or at least that's the plan, right?

Learning is how we build the skills we need for the next time. It allows us to know what to expect and gets us that much closer to becoming an expert.

When you got that first job or maybe your first job in your new career field you were a little bit nervous because you wanted to do well and prove to the world that you could do it.

I never want you to lose that little bit of nervousness because if you didn't truly have that little bit of nerves it would probably mean you were not "all in" on developing confidence.

I hope sharing my experience and a little bit about me gave you the courage and confidence to take on those fears.

All you need to do is to execute the plan that you have now created for yourself. It wouldn't hurt to have an accountability coach as well.

I can think of at least one..........ME!!

That's right, I would be honored to assist you in this journey of accountability to conquer your fears and gain that new confidence while taking on those new life challenges that come our way.

All you need to do is scan this QRL code by going to your camera on your smart phone and hover over the QRL code below and it will take you directly to my LinkedIn profile.

**David Alto**

LinkedIn ✨ content creator specializing 🏆 in getting your Resume past the ATS | LinkedIn...

Request to connect with me and write a little message about something you learned from reading my book and I will accept your connection request. After you finish with the accountability section you can even share it with me if you'd like. If you decide you need and want additional help, I'm just a message away.

# CHAPTER 9

# THE STORY, THE MYTH OF SISYPHUS

Greek mythology is filled with stories of the gods inflicting gruesome horrors on mortals who anger them.

Yet one of their most famous punishments is not remembered for its outrageous cruelty, but for its disturbing familiarity.

Sisyphus was the first king of Ephyra, now known as Corinth.

Although a clever ruler who made his city prosperous, he was also a devious tyrant who seduced his niece and killed visitors to show off his power.

This violation of the sacred hospitality tradition greatly angered the gods.

Finally, Zeus had enough and Sisyphus's punishment was a straightforward task – rolling a massive boulder up a hill.

But just as he approached the top, the rock would roll all the way back down, forcing Sisyphus to start over…and over, and over, for all eternity.

Historians have suggested that the tale of Sisyphus may stem from ancient myths about the rising and setting sun, or other natural cycles.

But the vivid image of someone condemned to endlessly repeat a futile task has resonated as an allegory about the human condition.

Existentialist philosopher Albert Camus compared the punishment to humanity's futile search for meaning and truth in a meaningless and indifferent universe.

Instead of despairing, Camus imagined Sisyphus defiantly meeting his fate as he walks down the hill to begin rolling the rock again.

And even if the daily struggles of our lives sometimes seem equally repetitive and absurd, we still give them significance and value by embracing them as our own.

I shared this story with you today to make sure you give your Fear significance. Embrace that this Fear is real.

But you don't need to go it alone. Once you successfully roll your personal rock up the hill to success, this shall too will pass.

If you give your Fear significance and realize it could take some time to roll your personal rock up that hill you will not have to suffer for eternity like Sisyphus.

Each time you recognize and embrace your Fear your rock with inch ever so much closer to the top.

Each time to allow yourself to feal pride you will gain the strength to move your rock.

By accepting what happen - allowing yourself time to collect your thoughts, and journaling your experience you will have the will and the strength to do what Sisyphus couldn't do.

I take the belief that it wasn't the fact that Sisyphus couldn't successfully push the rock up the hill, but that he was so arrogant that he lacked the mental maturity to grow and learn from his mistakes and failures.

You on the other hand have the mental strength and humility to get through anything life puts in front of you, even messing up on your first paid speaking engagement.

As a leader in social change, Dr. E. Beverly Young shares her thoughts on Fear.

*"To manage the debilitating effects of fear, I have to acknowledge that fear does not discriminate and usually without warning. If the fear is about events, I become motivated to uncover WHY I am fearful. If I believe the fear will affect me personally, I sometimes inadvertently allow it to become overwhelming and withdrawn."*

*"However, when I momentarily withdraw (no specific length of time), step back and step outside me, I discover that I fear (show reverence to) God more than the fear of rejection or lack of support or loneliness itself."*

*"I am more motivated to remain in the fight to make sense of my fear. I gain confidence, not arrogance, in the one who remains constant and who will help me confront my fears, God. My confidence in my only abilities are then strengthened."*

***Dr. E. Beverly Young***

Life is way too short to allow fear to rule us and I hope you now have a better understanding of how to attack that fear when it arrives, because it will and when it does you're going to attack it head on and with a smile.

I hope you make the rest of your week, your Best Week Ever.

*The End*

*FYI, I always wanted to write that...*

# YOUR HOMEWORK
# MY COMMITMENT

If you took the time to answer the questions in this book you now can enter each of those into the link below and have all of your answers all in one place. With those answers you will have a daily plan of attack to battle Fear and increase Confidence.

You can share your answers with me if you choose and I will be happy to be your accountability coach.

**Fear and Confidence engagement link:**

**My LinkedIn profile link:**

https://www.linkedin.com/in/davidalto/

**My email:**

davidalto@altoadvance.com

**My website:**

www.AltoAdvance.com

# ACKNOWLEDGEMENTS

"I would like to thank my wife, **Jen**. Thank you – I love you."

*"Thank you to my following friends for your contribution to my book on the subject of Fear, Confidence, and Impostor Syndrome."*

*"I recommend not only the services that each of them provides, I highly recommend connecting with them on LinkedIn because they are each very genuine in what they do."*

**Jean Tien**, for your tips on Fear., page 16

Jean is an intuitive mindset coach, specializing in working with ambitious, career driven women, who are ready to achieve more in life, as well as find balance and fulfillment. She uses her intuitive abilities, as well as her own extensive corporate experience, to help women find their Zone of Genius, fully align with it so they can powerfully bring it into the world.
Check out Jean on LinkedIn at the following link:
https://www.linkedin.com/in/jean-tien/

**Ashwini Prasad**, for your tips on Fear., page 17, 18

Ashwini is a relationship builder through her work as an Agile Coach, strategic business developer, IT project manager (cloud-based solutions). She is a PROSCI-certified Change Management Consultant and also known as The Inclusive Screenwriter, and leads with equity and justice as her pillars in her work as an anti-racist educator and screenwriter.
Check out Ash on LinkedIn at the following link:
https://www.linkedin.com/in/ashwiniprasad00/

**Beth Crosby**, for your tips on Fear., page 18

Beth empowers women to recognize that their unique story and experience help them build rapport with their ideal clients and make them the obvious choice. She is able to help women in this way through her proven process of interviewing, listening, brainstorming, and coaching them to write articles and posts relevant to their businesses.
Check out Beth on LinkedIn at the following link:
https://www.linkedin.com/in/bethcrosby/

**Christopher Salem**, for your tips on Fear., page 19

Christopher is an CEO, Executive Coach, Corporate Trainer, and Professional Speaker working with companies to create an interdependent work environment and thriving culture through a growth mindset foundation, effective communication, transparent leadership, and higher engagement.
Check out Christopher on LinkedIn at the following link: https://www.linkedin.com/in/christophersalem/

**Gary J. Lanham**, for your tips on Fear., page 19

Gary is an experienced manager, trainer, and speaker. He has worked over three decades in management, analyst, and other roles with leading companies in cash logistics and financial services. Gary regularly publishes inspiring and motivating content on LinkedIn in various formats, which includes 24 articles.
Check out Gary on LinkedIn at the following link:
https://www.linkedin.com/in/gilanham/

**Hilary Russo**, for your tips on Fear., page 19, 20

Hilary Russo, The HIListically Speaking™ Health Coach Certified Havening Techniques® Practitioner, Certified Holistic Health Coach and Health/Wellness Journalist.
Check out Hilary on LinkedIn at the following link:
https://www.linkedin.com/in/hilaryrusso/

**Phillip Yacinthe**, for your tips on Fear., page 20

Phillip is passionate about helping people in various capacities. Phillip has over 10 years' experience working various roles for several organizations focused on improving local communities. Extensive experience providing personal and professional development as well as life coaching for individuals particularly youth in mentorship roles.
Check out Phillip on LinkedIn at the following link:
https://www.linkedin.com/in/phillip-yacinthe-mba/

**Judy McCutcheon**, for your tips on Fear., page 21

Judy is an organizational redesign consultant, #Badass Impact Coach, helps women find their voice, Thrive Global Contributor, John Maxwell Certified Speaker, Teacher, Trainer, and Coach.
Check out Judy on LinkedIn at the following link:
https://www.linkedin.com/in/judy-mccutcheon/

**Chopra**, How Music Relieves Stress and Helps You Relax,.
page 22, 23

How Music Relives Stress and Helps You Relax
Chopra is the original integrative health experts blending modern well- being practices with Ayurveda system of health and healing.
Chopra main website: https://chopra.com/

**University of Nevada**, Reno -Counseling Services webpage.,
page 22

Releasingstressthroughmusic
I searched the internet for articles and publications regarding how music can help reduce stress and found the above referenced article to be most aligned with my experience.
The University of Nevada, Reno offers Counseling Services to students of the university to support and facilitate their personal and academic success and development.
University of Nevada, Reno main website: https://www.unr.edu/

**Sips by**, for your Tea suggestions for Stress & Anxiety., page 23

Sips by is a female-founded and led startup that makes discovering tea fun, personalized, and affordable. The Sips by Box is the only multi-brand, personalized tea subscription box. Each month, they match tea drinkers across the U.S. with delicious teas from over 150 global tea brands that their sure you'll love.
Check them out on Facebook at the following link:
https://www.facebook.com/sipsby/

**Doc Bruno Gervasi**, for your tips on Fear., page 24,25

Bruno is the owner of P2Fitness helping busy people lose weight the right way. Trainer, Coach/Virtual Coach providing 1 on 1 Professional Support and Guidance making your results as close to guaranteed as possible.
Check out Bruno on LinkedIn at the following link:
https://www.linkedin.com/in/dr-bruno/

**Victor Hallock**, for sharing your journey through Gratitude., page 25

Victor is a freelance writer for personal development, mindset coaches and speakers. He shares their message with their voice in a way that provides consistent value that is acted on.
Check out Victor on LinkedIn at the following link:
https://www.linkedin.com/in/victorhallock/

**Corrie LoGiudice**, for your tips on Fear., page 26

Corrie is a business strategist, coach, professional motivational speaker, host, influencer, and motivational maven. Corrie now works to help people profit from their passions and achieve freedom and balance through entrepreneurship. She also has been featured in TEDx, the Mighty, Authority Magazine, Thrive Global, Elite Daily, Girlboss, HelloGiggles, the Everygirl, Insider & Business Insider.
Check out Corrie on LinkedIn at the following link:
https://www.linkedin.com/in/iamcorrielo/

**Remo Chhetri**, for your tips on Fear., page 25 and your tips on Confidence., page 38

Remo has a recent MBA in HR-Marketing and is still searching for his dream job. Remo shares inspiring, thought provoking LinkedIn posts with his network and is an amazing giving individual and friend.
Check out Remo on LinkedIn at the following link:
http://www.linkedin.com/in/remochhetri/

**Lesley Osborn**, for your tips on Fear., page 26

Lesley founded Lesley Osborn Canine Consulting to provide education and guidance on fostering, adopting and caring for adult, senior, and special needs dogs. Focusing on "Quality of their Lives".
Check out Lesley on LinkedIn at the following link:
https://www.linkedin.com/in/lesley-osborn/

**Wikipedia**, referenced Impostor Syndrome definition., page 29

https://en.wikipedia.org/wiki/Impostor_syndrome
Wikipedia is an online free-content encyclopedia project helping to create a world in which everyone can freely share in the sum of all knowledge.
Wikipedia's main website:
https://en.wikipedia.org/wiki/Main_Page

**Joe Apfelbaum**, for your tips on Fear & Impostor Syndrome., page 33, 34

Joe is the CEO of Ajax Union, B2B Digital Marketing Agency in Brooklyn, NY
Helping B2B Companies w/Marketing Funnels. Joe is a LinkedIn Trainer, Speaker, Author and friend.
Check out Joe on LinkedIn at the following link:
https://www.linkedin.com/in/joeapfelbaum/

**Heather L. Picken,** for your tips on Journaling., page 35, 36

Heather is the CEO of Lux analytics and the inventor of the Vision Journal and creator of The Vision Method. The Vision Method is a new and revolutionary patent-pending journaling method that re-organizes your thoughts, expands your mind, and up level your business utilizing cutting edge neuroscience. Heather works with experienced entrepreneurs who are feeling stuck with their sales and blocked in their business to confident cash flow with more ease and less hustle. Her work in organizations focuses on growth mindset and creating energized employees.
Website: www.HeatherPicken.com
Website: www.Lux.Vision
Check out Heather on LinkedIn at the following link:
https://www.linkedin.com/in/heatherpicken/

**Cory Warfield**, for your tips on Fear & Confidence., page 39

Cory is a waiter turned entrepreneur. Now the Chief Visionary Officer of ShedWool. ShedWool has helped revolutionize the way businesses in over a dozen industries connect their employees to each other and their work schedules through their customizable web and mobile apps.
Check out Cory on LinkedIn at the following link:
https://www.linkedin.com/in/corywarfield/

**Josh Cole**, for your tips on Confidence & Failing., page 40, 41

Josh has been a peer, mentee, mentor, and good friend for over a decade.
Josh is a very giving Leader that continues to get amazing results from the various teams he has led because he always looks for opportunities to train and develop the individual. Josh, I couldn't have written my first book without mentioning a quote from you.
Check out Josh on LinkedIn at the following link:
https://www.linkedin.com/in/jcole1980/

**Gene Girdley,** for your tips on Confidence., page 43, 45

Gene is the Founder & President of DelRae Learning & Development.
Gene is a retail automotive professional and an experienced educator, trainer and friend. His diverse background includes sales, finance and fixed operations management, as well as in-dealership and on-camera, product and process training.
Check out Gene on LinkedIn at the following link:
https://www.linkedin.com/in/genegirdley/

**Jonaed Iqbal**, for your tips on Confidence., page 44, 45

I appreciate you for giving me my first guest appearance on a podcast.
You made the experience so amazing I now have been a guest on about 12+ podcasts and look to do more in the future. Thank you.
Jonaed is the founder and CEO of NoDegree.com and host of the NoDegree Podcast. Jonaed helps those without college degrees find meaningful jobs and is looking to change the landscape of those who choose an alternate route.
Check out Jonaed on LinkedIn at the following link:
https://www.linkedin.com/in/jonaed/

**Anthony English**, for your detailed tips on Confidence., page 46, 47

Anthony teaches self-employed people how to get comfortable with the tools and the mindset they need to run a business. He and his wife live in Australia and they have 7 children.
Check out Anthony on LinkedIn at the following link:
https://www.linkedin.com/in/anthonyenglish/

**Dr. E. Beverly Young**, for sharing your take on both Fear and Confidence., page 60

Beverly strives to change the narrative about police service by promoting Social Change through Training & Education and the founder and executive director of EbevyYG Learning Solutions, LLC.
Check out Beverly on LinkedIn at the following link:
https://www.linkedin.com/in/dr-e-beverly-young-a28750129/

I searched the internet for articles and publications regarding Confidence and found the work of **GoodTherapy®** to be the most aligned with my experience. Millions of people use GoodTherapy to find therapists and counselors, rehab and residential treatment centers, and mental health resources. If you or someone you know is experiencing mental health or behavioral concerns, relationship, relationship issues, or other challenges, search their directory to find a qualified therapist near you.

GoodTherapy believes that with the right support, anyone is capable of healing, growth, and change. Whether you're interested in mental health services or you provide them, you've come to the right place with GoodTherapy.

This book references the GoodTherapy ® article simply named "Confidence". https://www.goodtherapy.org/blog/psychpedia/confidence

Check out the GoodTherapy website: https://www.goodtherapy.org/about-us.html

I searched the internet for articles and publications regarding Fear and found the work of **Theo Tsaousides, Ph.D., ABPP** to be the most aligned with my experience and the message, I wanted to portray.

Theo is a neuropsychologist, author, and speaker. He specializes in the neuroscience of success, the brain science of goal Achievement. He helps his clients reach high levels of mental fitness using evidence-based practices from neuroscience, psychology, and brain training, so they can excel as high performers in their respective professional and personal roles.

---

This book references Theo's article "7 Things you Need to Know About Fear." You can read the entire article at the link below.
7 Things You Need to Know About Fear

**You might find these articles of Theo's very useful:**

"Why Are We Scared of Public Speaking?
Why Are We Scared of Public Speaking?

"Why Fear of Failure Can Keep You Stuck"
Why Fear of Failure Can Keep You Stuck

Check out Theo's website:
https://www.dr-theo.com/

Check out this reference to all of Theo's articles:
https://muckrack.com/theo-tsaousides-ph-d/articles

Check out Theo on LinkedIn at the following link:
https://www.linkedin.com/in/theotsaousides/

And then there is **Christian Jones** or his friends get to call him, Chris. I hired Chris in early 2020 to create a unique LinkedIn Banner for me. I wanted something unique to my serious yet playful approach to life and Chris nailed it. When I found out Chris could help me out with my website I knew I had the right guy. Thank you, Chris, for introducing me to the story of Sisyphus and your friendship. Oh yes, Chris created my book design as well as my new LinkedIn Banner. Major props. LinkedIn is more than a place for recruiters and jobseekers. LinkedIn is a place to forge B2B relationships and true friendships even from across the pond. We call Chris a visual design Jedi. Chris specializes in professional editorial or corporate PowerPoint illustrations for anything you can imagine.

Check out Chris on LinkedIn at the following link:
https://www.linkedin.com/in/glenn-christian-cook-jones/

---

Thank you **Mark R. Morris Jr** for providing the editing and creative suggestions/edits for this book.

Mark provides the following services: Book Ghostwriter - Blog Ghostwriter - Book writing coach - Publishing coach - Writing and publishing consultation – Article Ghostwriter – Website Copywriter – LinkedIn Ghostwriter

Check out Mark on LinkedIn at the following link:
https://www.linkedin.com/in/markrmorrisjr-ghostwriter/

BIG shout out to **Dave Officer** for creating my amazing logo of me battling the evil ATS (Applicant – Tracking – System) resume bots.

Dave is a freelance designer and illustrator who has been honing his craft in logo design, visual identity and illustration for the past 15 years.

Check out Dave on LinkedIn at the following link:
https://www.linkedin.com/in/david-officer/

---

# ABOUT THE AUTHOR

David Alto provides Resume, LinkedIn, and Interview Coaching specializing in getting his clients resumes past the evil resume bots. David's articles have been published on MarketWatch, Daily Herald - Suburban Chicago's Information Source, SNN, Fox34 News, NCN, and WBOC CBS.

David empowers and promotes the talents and experiences of those looking to accomplish their career goals and excel in their profession.

His positioning statement "**Advancing business with personal solutions**."

David's clients, past, present and future are the inspiration, and his true passion.

When David's not helping clients, you can find him and interact with him on the amazing platform of LinkedIn.

---

*There is no better feeling in life then to unselfishly help another without asking for anything in return.*

---

www.ingramcontent.com/pod-product-compliance
Lightning Source LLC
LaVergne TN
LVHW050609100826
845148LV00015B/3196

* 9 7 8 1 7 1 6 3 0 0 7 0 7 *